2500-Plus Helpful Ideas

IMPROVED EDITION

Gary Borisen

2500-Plus Helpful Ideas

IMPROVED EDITION

Gary Russell Borisen

 ISBN 978-1-387- 56566-5

Table of Contents

Dedication

This book is of some of my experiences and could have been experiences of helpful ideas, and dedicated to Mayor Donald Fracassi, my Father, Mother, two brothers, sister, son Jeff Borisen helped me with revising some parts of this book, daughter, grandson, five granddaughters, also three great-grand boys, three great-grand girls, and divorcee with her parent's.

Autobiography

I use capitalization and or underlining to emphasize throughout my book. My Grandfather Thomas Trofim Borisenko on my Father's side, Lydia Eulita Tuchin and their two children came from the northwest farm area of the Black Sea from Russia to the Port of Halifax, Nova Scotia Canada 4-20-1912 on the SS-Victorian Steam Ship. They homesteaded at Rabbit Lake Saskatoon, Saskatchewan in the Arelee District to farm wheat on W. 6-38-11 W3 a plot of land of 600 acres and leased 400 acres, had a family of ten children, and later moved to Toronto, Ontario in 1938 where they had two small restaurants. My grandfather and his oldest son had 40-acre farms of fruit next to each other of black cherries, peaches, pears, apples, plums, grapes, some vegetables, and a few chickens in Niagara Falls. My Mother Margaret Kathleen Rossiter was born in 1920 in Montreal, Quebec Canada, and when she was older she got a job as a waitress in Toronto, Ontario and fell in love with the owner Ely Jack Borisenko of a small restaurant, and they married. My parents took their children to visit many relatives and on other vacations.

I was born in Canada in 1944, my parents moved to Detroit, Michigan in 1946 where I attended kindergarten, and the first grade as the second oldest son. My parents and their four children moved to Southfield in 1951. I studied in the Birmingham Schools where did NOT get mentoring, counseling, or tutoring, and should not have graduated from high school in 1963 because the principal said I could stay another year (reading was done continuously from the front cover to the back cover in the 9-th grade. I took a study skills course in 1998), because of this Unfair Deceptive Cold Stained Busy System of Things which is: NOT GETTING GOOD information, advice, EDUCATION, mentoring, counseling, tutoring, or follow-up EARLY IN LIFE and later on, being uninformed, DECEPTION, greed, verbal and physical abuse, LACK OF BETTER EDUCATION, COMMUNICATIONS, religion, ethics, time, money, and love!

I was employed at six small drafting companies for two years as a manual tooling fixture drafter. I worked for a machinist leader as his helper and as a machinist for five months at a fixture machine company. I was employed at Chevrolet Motor Division for ten years as a manual V8-Engine Chassis Drafting Detailer. I was employed at the Ford Motor Company as a Product Design Engineer for 13 years in Interior and Exterior Trim Engineering, studied their engineering training program, and other courses. I worked at Farmer Jack Shopping Center as a cashier for six years fulltime because of this Unfair Deceptive Cold Stained Busy System of Things, the five-year fashioned divorce, and not working at the Ford Motor Company as a Product Design Engineer!

I took three yearly educational leaves of absents from Chevrolet Motor Division, and worked 14 months during those educational leaves at some of those small drafting companies of the 24 months because needed money. I studied at three: adult education centers, college extension centers, community colleges, universities, and worked some. I graduated from Oakland Community College with an Associate in Arts of Pre-Engineering April of 1969. I barely graduated from Wayne State University with a Bachelor of Mechanical Engineering Technology Degree June of 1977 while being married with two children and working full-time at Chevrolet. I learned how to type, and to read a better way with a study skills course finally at the age of fifty-four in 1998 at a junior college during the last year of college courses where my semester three credit two courses grade point doubled from high school.

I was married for 17 years plus five divorcing years, we got divorced because of this Unfair Deceptive Cold Stained Busy System of Things. We have a son, daughter, six grandchildren, and six great-grandchildren. I had a Residential Real Estate License for 17 years but only worked equivalent to one year part-time. I did 60 hours of private dance lessons, 300 hours of group lessons, and wrote 160 half pages of dance notes from 6 dance studios and 14 dance clubs after the divorce. I am retired in a small old mobile home doing minor repairs, some of the maintenance, chores, minor exercising, and reading only what has to be read.

2003

About the Author

I use capitalization and or underlining to emphasize throughout my book. I worked at the friendly Kroger Shopping Center for 15 months from June of 1962 to September of 1963, did not sign a union pension card on the last day of work while fantasizing and assuming where usually the devil is because became a draftsman, and did not receive compensation from the United Food and Commercial Workers International Union-Industry Pension Fund for my union dues paid! My 15 months if added to the Farmer Jack Pension would be more like it!

I injured my lower back in 1966 from three high dives into Stony Lake in Oxford, Michigan and went to 20 doctors during 53 years because of back pain. Since young kids were doing high dives I felt as if could do them and dove into the water a third time with my hands and feet apart because did not know that my hands and feet should touch together, came to the surface and could not feel the lower part of my body. I used my hands only to swim back to the diving raft, laid on my back and could not feel the lower part of my body for a few minutes, and now avoid exercising and twisting of the lower spine. I was employed at Chevrolet Motor Division as a manual V8-Engine Chassis Drafting Detailer sitting down while not wanting the employer to know about my back injury thinking it might get better.

I went to a medical physical therapist doctor at Royal Oak Beaumont Hospital in 1976 because of the high diving injury, the medical doctor said if my disk were on an angle of five degrees more that I would not be able to walk again. Cardiology and Vascular Associates, P. C. Echocardiogram

3-11-2000 report, there is mitral valve prolapse (born with a heart murmur) with mild to moderate aortic and pulmonary insufficiency. A MRI X-ray 5-13-2010 at Basha Diagnostics, P, C. revealed a herniated lower disc L5-S1 and I still have some excessive back pain for two days when doing different kinds of manual labor. Beaumont Hospital 11-16-2012 mild tortuous aorta (probably from the diving injury) chest PA/AP lateral two views, ribs unilateral right two views without chest.

I went thru a five-year fashioned divorce 1987 to 1992, not working at the Ford Motor Company while being unemployed for eight years 1990-1998 while in a divorce, because some people (wife) are brain washed to DESTROY you instead of helping you. I was employed at the Farmer Jack Shopping Center fulltime as a cashier for six years (with right arm pit area pain from repetitive movement of the right arm from scanning groceries 1998 to 2004), because of this Unfair Deceptive Cold Stained Busy System of Things!

I had more injuries while needing something to do while in a five year fashioned divorce, because of Fidelity Brokerage Services, and while not working at the Ford Motor Company for eight years. My diving injury of back pain is just enough to mess-up my life because of this Unfair Deceptive Cold Stained Busy System of Things which is: NOT GETTING GOOD information, advice, EDUCATION, mentoring, counseling, tutoring, or follow-up EARLY IN LIFE and later on, being uninformed, DECEPTION, greed, verbal and physical abuse, LACK OF BETTER EDUCATION, COMMUNICATIONS, religion, ethics, time, money, and love! I lost a lot of money to the Michigan State Lottery and the Invention Submissions Corporation with a widget invention idea while trying to get an easier source of money while fantasizing and assuming where usually the devil is, because of more injuries while needing an easier way to make money and something to do

while being unemployed for eight years with the fashioned divorce proceedings.

I lost my job as a Product Design Engineer from the Ford Motor Company because of this Unfair Deceptive Cold Stained Busy System of Things, injuries, and the fashioned divorce proceedings! Two engineering companies hired me and then they let me go after a couple of weeks while in a divorce. I went to TWELVE different kinds of sort of marriage counselors and NOBODY did anything constructive for me about my marriage as if do NOT exist, and TWELVE out of THIRTEEN relationships in my family ended in divorces presently! If you do not want to get divorced do not get married. People are usually brain washed to destroy somebody instead of helping them. People that want to get married could: do-good Bible STUDIES with their parents early in life for five years and then longer, and in the schools, learn to read a better way with a study skills course, write a better way, study an ANGER MANAGEMENT COURSE, get MENTORED, earn a college degree of interest, WAIT for somebody equal to so there is less arguments, and become TWENTY-EIGHT years of age when the brain is mostly developed?

A spouse can file for a divorce while fantasizing and assuming where usually the devil is with false pretense anytime! A spouse can drag their husband through the court system with seven attorneys for five years that take what both worked for 20 years, because of this Unfair Deceptive Cold Stained Busy System of Things, and a human sparked inadvertent computer error from Fidelity Brokerage Services W362135-30NOV17! There must be something WRONG with this Unfair Deceptive Cold Stained Busy System of Things, SCHOOL SYSTEMS, MARRIAGE COUNSELORS, DIVORCE LAWS, religious organizations, and fashioned spouses! Life is about aches, pains, and suffering, because some

people (wife) are brain washed from TV and other people to DESTROY you instead of helping you.

This book is of SOME OF MY EXPERIENCES AND COULD HAVE BEEN EXPERIENCES OF HELPFUL IDEAS started May 13, 2007 for family, and May 27 for the Jehovah's Witnesses Sunday Service. I answered a question from the weekly reading by microphone as a new person like the other people, but then added my first FAMILY HELPFUL IDEA. My Jehovah's Witness sponsor told me two weeks later that should not say the family helpful idea because only Bible STUDIES. I did some Bible STUDIES at home May of 2007 to November of 2011 with two Jehovah's Witnesses. I decided to do the September of 2013 handwritten 65 pages of 486 ideas as a book started February of 2014 to HELP MY FAMILY, improve my English skills, and IMPROVE this Unfair Deceptive Cold Stained Busy System of Things!

I read and studied *Microsoft Word 2013 for Dummies* 2013 a computer book of 400 pages. *The Answer Book* 1993 an English book of 375 pages as a reference manual for office personnel from the Ford Motor Company. *The Business Writer's Handbook* 1976 as a reference book of 575 pages. *Webster's Illustrated Contemporary Dictionary* 1988, *Webster's Collegiate Thesaurus* 1976, *Webster's New World Dictionary and Thesaurus* 1996, and *Webster's New World Portable Large Print Dictionary* 2007. I read a paragraph about my grandfather on my Father's side from *Reflections* 1982 compiled by the Arelee District and the Historical Association of Arelee Saskatoon, Saskatchewan Canada a book of 400 pages. I read sections of Microsoft Word 2016 for Dummies 2016, and Word 2016 in easy steps 2016. I applied the books to my document of 19,715 words by using the computer Microsoft Office 2016 with Word at the friendly library which is more

than my prior paper of 3,800 words and have been looking at DVDS from the library at home since 2009 now and then.

Contents

I use capitalization and or underling to emphasize throughout my book. When there is a calling it is time to do some writing! EVERYBODY CAN PROFIT FROM THE VARIETY OF THE DIVERSIFICATION of some of these many HELPFUL IDEAS, some more, some less depending on their experiences in life. These IDEAS are to inform of SOME OF MY INVOLVEMENTS AND COULD HAVE BEEN EXPERIENCES OF MORE THAN ONE IDEA FOR MOST OF THE PARAGRAPHS of chapters of Money, Safety, Health, Family, and Other HELPFUL IDEAS in this Unfair Deceptive Cold Stained Busy System of Things which is: NOT GETTING GOOD information, advice, EDUCATION, mentoring, counseling, tutoring, or follow-up EARLY IN LIFE, being uninformed, DECEPTION, greed, verbal and physical abuse, LACK OF BETTER EDUCATION, COMMUNICATIONS, religion, ethics, time, money, and love! THE SCHOOLS COULD HAVE A MENTORING COURSE AT AN EARLY AGE TO IMPROVE the system AND BE MENTORED EARLY and in the SENIOR YEAR!

Everybody has different experiences in life from what mentoring, counseling, tutoring, advice, information, and follow-up they got at an early age IF ANY! Verbal abuse can be just as bad as physical abuse, and if not knowing what to do and say do NOT do or say anything, unless it is helpful! Newton's Law of Action, basically for every action there is a reaction, and for EVERY SOCIAL ACTION THERE IS A SOCIAL REACTION NOW AND OR IN THE FUTURE! If you are fantasizing and assuming you are usually gambling with the devil instead of the real environment. People should have a BETTER chance in the world if living in the educational state of mind that is the educational material from the schools and libraries, and the spiritual state of mind that is good Bible

2500-Plus Helpful Ideas: Contents

STUDIES like in a class with their parents early in life for five years and then longer, and in the schools.

Chapters

2500-Plus Helpful Ideas

Chapter 1 Money Helpful Ideas

PEOPLE SHOULD CHECK WITH QUALIFIED ORGANIZATIONS WITH THEIR PEOPLE FOR ADVICE.

I use capitalization and or underlining to emphasize throughout my book. Everybody has different experiences in life from what mentoring, counseling, tutoring, advice, information, and follow-up they got at an early age IF ANY in this UNFAIR DECEPTIVE COLD STAINED BUSY SYSTEM OF THINGS which is: NOT GETTING GOOD information, advice, EDUCATION, mentoring, counseling, tutoring, or follow-up EARLY IN LIFE and later on, being uninformed, DECEPTION, greed, verbal and physical abuse, LACK OF BETTER EDUCATION, COMMUNICATIONS, religion, ethics, time, money, and love! THE SCHOOLS COULD HAVE A MENTORING COURSE AT AN EARLY AGE TO IMPROVE the system AND BE MENTORED EARLY and in the SENIOR YEAR!

Somebody could STRETCH some old clothes from the black rack a little by putting an item on a doorknob and pulling on the item CAUTIOUSLY, and use some of those clothes longer, but do not let a close friend see doing that which is a very real big important significant thing for a few particular interested observables.

Someone could buy some larger size clothes because they do shrink some, might gain some weight, and could use low heat instead of high in the dryer. Sterling Heights Public Library DVD j372.4 BETWEEN THE LIONS, Poetry Day, Oh Yes It Can (as red, light brown, and yellow-checkered extra-large stylish Arty Smarty Dance Pants for smarty people).

Chapter 1 Money Helpful Ideas

Someone could READ a book about Wills from the library, use an old Will as reference and programmable computer discs to fill in the blanks, type in the blanks for a Will, Durable Financial Power of Attorney, and Designation of Patient Advocate and Living Will, might ask some free legal aid questions, print four copies each, and have them notarized at the city hall. Someone could designate beneficiaries at the bank for accounts and give a copy of the legal papers to the beneficiaries later.

Somebody might get a suggestion award if having a good suggestion for their employer. Someone could put some investments in a CREDIT UNION instead of the company where working in case changing to a different company. Someone could remove some of the old hardware from damaged things not used and save the hardware in case needed for a future use, and might save a gift that do not want for somebody else.

I removed pages that like from a flower bouquet magazine, put some of them into picture frames, and mounted some of them on the walls. I got things ready a few days before going somewhere and added other things as needed. I was in a hotel room while getting ready to check out, did not look into all the draws, closets, and cupboards while fantasizing and assuming where usually the devil is, and LEFT MY Minolta Camera with a flash attachment, camera case, film, and pictures in the camera in a nightstand in the room!

Someone could try to pay for everything new or used, rent, borrow, or wait, try NOT to pay anybody any interest or fees, and might not give any money away unless all bills and debts are paid while having a healthy checking and savings account. People should read and STUDY papers carefully at home before signing because they might discover about things not knowing and overpay upfront, might pay fully for small things, and over time for real estate, mobile home, vehicle, motorhome, attractive boat, in-ground swimming pool, Jacuzzi hot tub, home repairs and furnishings.

People could EARN A COLLEGE DEGREE in an area of interest that will be useful to help in life when unemployed and need money. Students that get LESS than a "B" in school should get TUTORING and try to stay in the schools to get educated! Parents might have to support their kids when they get older if they do not get educated EARLY a better way. Some colleges have financial discounts for some degrees of study with various types of guaranteed job employment after graduation, and graduates might become employed in an area of interest that they would personally like to benefit from.

People that earn a MASTER'S DEGREE in the accounting or stock market area could study DVDS about finances, listen to the AM radio, and watch TV about the stock market. Somebody might work as a stockbroker and put a large amount of money into the bank before investing in the stock market, wait when things are favorable for investing, and try to use proper judgment. Somebody might wait for the next short bear market sometime one month before the selling price goes up, and should NOT put all investments in one place while fantasizing and assuming where usually the devil is.

IF IT DOES NOT FEEL RIGHT IN YOUR HEART AND SOUL SHOULD NOT DO IT! Someone might invest with family or relatives instead of somebody else. People should try to hold onto what money they have, and spend wisely. Organizations asking for donations usually use some of the money for their vacations and toys. Someone should study money track DVDS from the friendly library because EVERYBODY AND EVERYTHING ARE DECEPTIVE SOME OR WORSE!

People might try to stay free of legal ties from loans, pledges, donations, and any other financial ties, and should try to answer and resolve a problem fast if getting a legal paper. Gambling is DECEPTIVE and can lead to losses, mental illness, reckless things, theft, or even suicide because of this Unfair Deceptive Cold Stained Busy System of Things!

Somebody should not have left important personal bank papers about a few people in their vehicle for years! The only two people you can usually trust are the parents, but that depends on the current conditions. If you give somebody a financial task or decision to do of your finances they might NOT do it right and you will suffer! If you want something done of yours the way you want it done do it yourself! You can save money by doing things yourself so get educated throughout life.

People should listen to their INNERSOLE because a setback might be a setup for quick action, and if not wanting to make a quick important financial decision could say, I will get back with you. Someone might use a tape recorder and or verbally repeat back their important written information for the verification of the information.

People should make a monthly average INCOME SHEET and update the sheet as needed! Incomes from: Social Security, pensions, health reimbursements, insurance, Federal, State, and City Income Taxes, bank interest, loans,

investments, credit card reward points cash back, gifts, dinners, organizations, food stamps, and miscellaneous.

People should make a monthly average EXPENSE SHEET and update the sheet as needed! Expenses for: Federal, State, City, School, and Real Estate Taxes, Social Security, mortgage, rent, utilities, home insurance, repairs, and furnishings, loans, investments, debit, credit, and store charge cards, medical, prescription, dental, and optical insurances, and miscellaneous.

Expenses for: vehicle payments, auto insurance, fuel, regular auto repairs and upgrades, vehicle damage, parking and toll fees, driver's license and registration, groceries, restaurants, toiletries, clothing, stores, haircuts, stationery, postage stamps and mailing charges, social dinners, entertainment, vacations, hobbies, tips, gifts, misplaced and lost items, donations, home theft items, tobacco, alcohol, drugs, gambling, illicit sex, reckless, and miscellaneous things.

People should make a SERVICE SHEET of the services they get percent value from 100 percent of rent and update the sheet as needed. Services from: City Hall, Homeland Security Advisory and Alert System, fire and police stations, emergency medical centers, hospitals, medical companies, fitness centers, stores, and restaurants.

Services from: Consumers Energy, Detroit Electric Energy, Internet, television, telephone, water, sewer, parking and road repairs, sweeping and snow plowing of streets, pickup of rubbish and large items, leaves, twigs in leaf bags, appliances, tree trimming and removal, spraying of weeds and lawn insects, and edging of mobile home park sidewalks.

Chapter 1 Money Helpful Ideas

Services from: residential location with local WEATHER CONDITIONS, family, relatives, friends, church, schools, colleges, adult education, library, computers, books, CDS, DVDS, brochures, income tax papers, Xerox copies, mailbox, clubhouse facilities, swimming pool, holiday festival celebrations, dance studio, community picnic, yard sale, guest parking, social organizations, and miscellaneous.

People could help block a check against identity theft from cashing the check by writing the MIDDLE NAME, mail it at the post office, and PREPARE for a financial downsizing because eventually something will happen! People could save slowly with secured smaller amounts which is usually better than gambling with a large amount of money, and put two years of money into the bank to live off of comfortably.

People that change to a different utility service company because they want to try to save some money might experience an expensive rate increase, and charged a large cancellation fee by their new provider if they change to another company. Automatic payments from a bank can REDUCE the amount of payment of auto and home insurances, and might close some small monthly payments and fees. People could make a detailed inventory of personal products and update it for their homeowner's insurance.

Someone could have Plan-A, if Plan-A does not work have Plan-B as backup, if Plan-B does not work have Plan-C as backup, and if Plan-C does not occur they could rethink plans. Someone might reduce the credit limits on store and credit charge cards and ask if would REDUCE their interest rates, use credit and store charge cards to get reward points, and a debit card for cash advances.

Chapter 1 Money Helpful Ideas

Someone should NOT rush when making an important financial decision because they might make a mistake, could comeback a different time with a friend to sign a document, draw lines thru the spaces in a contract if not using the blank lines for their peace of mind, and get two copies of all the papers signed.

Someone should CHECK receipts and change if fantasizing and assuming where usually the devil is, and could try to go as close to the originating source of a product to save some money. A product at a better discount is harder to get unless knowing somebody that owns part of a company and or is family related, or just a KIND friend. Somebody could call an appliance store if they bought the wrong color and size appliances to return them with receipts.

Somebody could have a SUNLAMP in case needed to thaw a vehicle door lock, trunk lock, frozen rain from the storage-shed lock, and ice in a steel bathtub U-pipe inside an old mobile home when the temperature is −17° F outside. Somebody could pack insulation around a forty-seven year-old bathtub U-pipe underneath the mobile home, add a closure board to cover the U-pipe, put the insulation back up under the mobile home where it has fallen down, and add insulation in other areas. People should buy ONLY what is needed because any more would be a waste of their hard-earned money and a loss from society.

Somebody might pay a NEIGHBOR to Rake the foliage from the top of the lawn, remove some thatch, plant grass seed, roll the lawn, cut, trim, and edge the grass by the sidewalk by pushing the soil back up off the cement, add landscaping soil, water, fertilize, rake, and mulch the fall leaves. Somebody could SOS-Pad clean five thirty-three year- old vehicle magnesium wheels, jumpstart a battery, paint the storage shed

foundation, replace a garbage disposal and reroute the drainage pipe, then shovel the snowfalls of two inches or more usually when it has stopped snowing.

To unlock a lock turn knob right THREE full turns and do not push or pull on shackle. Somebody might get a defective product REFUND if a colored frozen programmable combination lock requires four hard pulls on the shackle to open the lock. A store might take an item back that is over five years if having a legible receipt depending on the special reason, and get a raincheck for a queen-size mattress-heating pad with heat wires because of a medical letter of a back condition?

People could buy things during January, July, and at special sales to get some BETTER discounts, try on some nice clothes before buying them instead of by tag sizes, and might have clothes made to fit from a body scan. Somebody might buy men's clearance shirts regular $40 for $3 at a store from a clearance rack and use store points.

I should have SIGNED A UNION PENSION CARD for working a year at Kroger's United Food and Commercial Workers International Union-Industry as a cashier because I worked for that company again! I did NOT see a funeral procession when at a residential street stop sign, drove forward, beside the procession, and then turned into a parking lot. I GOT AN UNFAIR FINE because the judge never asked me if I have anything to say for myself, because of this Unfair Deceptive Cold Stained Busy System of Things!

People could buy real estate based on LOCATION during a buyers' market, BUY LOW, AND SELL HIGH, the purchaser could make a low offer, then the seller might

counter with a different price. Somebody could GO to a street where would like to buy a house or commercial property, talk to the owners and close neighbors, and might do some of the paperwork? Somebody could bring a clipboard and write the things that need to be repaired when reviewing real estate on the second visit and add them to the purchase agreement. The buyer could ATTACH an addendum to the purchase agreement if not enough room, and have the property APPRAISED by brick and mortar value, not by Wall Street Pricing Method based on sales talk during a sellers' market!

Somebody might buy a house from a family member, relative, estate sale, bankruptcy, auction, buy owner, or a real estate company. Home size is usually 500 square feet per person and 200 for outside storage space depending on their needs, could get advice before, and BRING a person of experience to help do important financial transactions. A mortgage payment should usually not be more than 25 percent of the take-home pay after payroll deductions. When your daughter and son are not cooperating with their previous experienced licensed real estate Father about buying real estate they will lose BIG TIME in the long run for 30 years about Wall Street Pricing Method of real estate based on sales talk during a sellers' market instead of the APPRAISED brick and mortar value, so rent instead until a buyers' market, or might buy by owner.

I bought a Microsoft Computer Book and an English book to STUDY them to use the computer at the friendly library. Computer systems are expensive to buy, update, and know how to operate. My granddaughter wrote a paper about an elegant giraffe named Ina, seven-year-old granddaughter scribbled a colorful seven-page paper about an elegant giraffe with pencil, crayons, and watercolors.

Chapter 1 Money Helpful Ideas

Somebody might develop a document a number of DIFFERENT focused ways of reading Xerox copies at home and working at a computer at the friendly library. The more times doing something the CLOSER to 100 percent you will get, ten small things equal a medium thing, and ten medium things equal a large noticeable change. Somebody could edit a document slowly silently or VERBALLY while sitting on a chair or standing, and read four different ways silent front to back, verbal front to back, silent back to front, and verbal back to front. Somebody could start to close out some paragraphs now and at the near end of editing to save some time until getting two silent and two verbal readings each close together without changes during this Unfair Deceptive Cold Stained Busy System of Things which is: NOT GETTING GOOD information, advice, EDUCATION, mentoring, counseling, tutoring, or follow-up EARLY IN LIFE and later on, being uninformed, DECEPTION, greed, verbal and physical abuse, LACK OF BETTER EDUCATION, COMMUNICATIONS, religion, ethics, time, money, and love!

Everybody can profit from the variety of the diversification of some of these many HELPFUL IDEAS, some more, some less depending on their experiences in life. You could do this, should do that, or you might do something else different, good luck.

Chapter 2 Safety Helpful Ideas

PEOPLE SHOULD CHECK WITH QUALIFIED ORGANIZATIONS WITH THEIR PEOPLE FOR ADVICE.

I use capitalization and or underlining to emphasize throughout my book. Everybody has different experiences in life from what mentoring, counseling, tutoring, advice, information, and follow-up they got at an early age IF ANY in this UNFAIR DECEPTIVE COLD STAINED BUSY SYSTEM OF THINGS which is: NOT GETTING GOOD information, advice, EDUCATION, mentoring, counseling, tutoring, or follow-up EARLY IN LIFE and later on, being uninformed, DECEPTION, greed, verbal and physical abuse, LACK OF BETTER EDUCATION, COMMUNICATIONS, religion, ethics, time, money, and love! THE SCHOOLS COULD HAVE A MENTORING COURSE AT AN EARLY AGE TO IMPROVE the system AND BE MENTORED EARLY and in the SENIOR YEAR!

Someone might PARK a vehicle if a heavy deep snowfall, snowsquall storm, black ice is on the road, cloudburst rainstorm, earthquake, or if a tornado is in the vicinity then stay LOW in the vehicle, or sit low in a corner inside a building (because was bad)? Someone should close the blinds and stay away from the windows during thunderstorms, strong winds, tornadoes, or if a rare bright loud meteorite. Somebody could avoid taking a shower which is not that hard to do, turnoff the colorful ultrahigh definition television, and SEEK shelter or might get injured if broken flying glass from the windows.

People could keep an important paper in the front trouser pocket instead of the top shirt pocket, because it might

come out with other things in the top shirt pocket. People could write a note on a calendar before forgetting something, put a note or an item on a table, or use a timer as the reminder. Somebody calls on the phone and wants to sell something and get their personal information, could tell him or her (I am having munchies now do not bother me), I will make the phone call if wanting to buy something, or have an answering machine!

A swindler with a long twisted upturned mustache might come to the home and say your shingles on the roof could use a repair, while the owner is going to the outside backyard to look, a burglar that is hiding with a small periscope could go into the home because of the unlocked front freebee door, and Rob the home or Worse! Burglars are working fast with high-tech tools and do not want to be SEEN or HEARD, and can cut a lock or chain within two to three minutes depending on the type of lock and chain, and do not encourage strangers to come onto your property!

A painting truck could park on the driveway when nobody is home, then a swindle painter with a colorful swindle painter's hat on could go to the backyard and look for an opened window on the second floor. Two burglars could come with painting outfits on and a burglar ladder to the private backyard, enter into the home thru an opened freebee window, and Rob the home or Worse, but somebody might have motion detectors inside the home for security, a security guard, and or a security dog!

People might put an address label on one side of a flash drive, scribe a phone number on the other side, scribe a letter on a short side, and initials on another side. People could add a file to a flash drive stating the owner and e-mail address, backup three flash drives with another file each for security,

and have another flash drive for archives. People could keep an eye on the flash drive when in a library and working at a computer, have ONLY what is needed at the time on the desk, and a light jacket on the back of the chair.

Some structures could be built on higher level ground on elevated long column posts on high foundations away from flood zones, some road surfaces could be built higher, and have more tsunami warning systems! There should be more HURRICANE ZONING LAWS for some structures on ocean coast lines to be built BETTER AND STRONGER on elevated long column posts, no basements or first floors, just round second, third, or fourth floors with round corners to category five hurricane level, or NOT built in certain areas because of local weather conditions and or hurricane zoning laws! There could be more relief centers every so many miles with water and food, and some people could move 400 miles away for a month or so before and after a hurricane, or permanently!

Structures of more than one level could have outside FIRE ESCAPE LADDERS AND OR STAIRS! Some communities could have FIRE ZONING LAWS for clearance of flat land vegetation from the community of a set distance of no vegetation. Some fireproof structures could be built in the center of four acres with no vegetation just lava rocks instead of grass, and have a large basement storm shelter underground. Some mountainous structures should NOT be built in some areas because of local weather conditions and or FIRE ZONING LAWS, and there could be more lookout towers of structures to be built better.

There should be more VOLCANO ZONING LAWS for structures NOT to be built in some areas of a volcano! The world will probably end up destroyed by pollution of all different kinds, fantasizing and assuming where usually the

devil is, DECEPTION, greed, mismanagement of money, social, verbal, and physical abuse, violence, theft, crimes, wars, storms, land, sea, and air pollution?

Somebody could wear a white shirt when constructing a sturdy metal storage-shed while working in the bright sun to be cooler, seal topside and underside of the leak areas to protect from heavy water leaks, and have TWO locks on the door facing a bedroom window! Someone should turn the window blinds a little to see the storage-shed door, tape two of the slats together at one end on an angle for the outside view, and then leave the blinds that way. Someone could pretend as a burglar and CHECK from the outside and inside of the home during the day and at night, windows, doors, flood and motion lights, cameras, exit ladders from second floor windows, then monitor them!

Somebody STOLE MY LAWN MOWER by snipping the one tenth of an inch-thick chain! Somebody should use different kinds of outside locks UP at the top with thick chains, outside regular bright lights, flood lights, security cameras, and motion sensing light bulbs which have a warranty. Some jewelry stores could have bulletproof cases instead of glass for their jewelry and a security guard with a zapper.

Once in a while I sit on one of the arm sleeves of my leather jacket at a restaurant and at other places so knowing where it is or might lose the jacket one of these days. Someone might REDUCE the noise before concentrating on a financial decision, ask questions of services, get two copies of the papers to read, and write penciled notes on one copy! Someone could say a number five times, write the number on a paper five times, and relate the number mentally to something else on a mental pegboard five times.

Chapter 2 Safety Helpful Ideas

People are usually safe when alone, and should NOT let anybody into the home unless knowing them for a long time and thinking that they will not harm them. Somebody might take something and damage some personal property if the babysitter or someone else invites somebody in, so be on the WATCH for unexpected strangers!

Somebody might knock on the side door and then you could tell him or her to go to the front door. Somebody should call the POLICE right away if three burglars come to the front door dressed as if the police with guns while they are fantasizing and assuming where usually the devil is because of this Unfair Deceptive Cold Stained Busy System of Things!

A senior lady behind me in a party store in line to pay set her large purse down, turned around to look at something, and then turned back where her purse was now GONE! People should hold onto their wallet or purse, wait to take their keys or money out UNTIL ready to use them, and right after using their keys or money put them away in a safe place! Someone could have a backup plan if no current key to unlock the mailbox, vehicle, home, storage shed, or office door.

People should protect from EVERYBODY and EVERYTHING at all times, because somebody will steal anything of value! I should have put my two rings into a pocket instead of on the counter so not forgetting them in a hospital restroom by the cafeteria while washing my hands and thinking of what to EAT. MY TWO RINGS WERE NOT in the lost and found where I left my phone number! If leaving your shopping cart with three paper bags worth FIFTEEN CENTS EACH as a credit unattended to get an item in the next isle when nobody is in your isle somebody might steal the shopping cart with the THREE PAPER BAGS, or could have a security guard to be with you throughout life!

Somebody with less might take things if bragging about them or just talking about them, and somebody running by might steal a cellular phone, so be on the WATCH! Somebody could get into trouble when volunteering to do something not qualified to do, might take a martial arts course for self-defense, and go on to another course. Someone might give somebody a complement and they might interpolate the complement as VERBAL ABUSE or might misunderstand if joking around, then somebody might suffer.

A solicitor could pull on the door handle if thinking nobody is home while putting a rolled paper with a rubber band on the door handle. Someone should have an optical peek ocular glass in a door to SEE who is on the other side. People do NOT have to open the screened door if solicitors come to the front door, they could tell them to put their papers into the mailbox, might say not interested thanks anyway, or might put two NO SOLICITORS signs in good viewing spots?

Someone could have a motion light for their porch light, outside motion and flood lights installed on the home and MANUALLY turn them on and off to let somebody outside know that seeing them, and in case a 911 Signal is needed! Someone might use some seven-watt light bulbs for better lighting for nightlights instead of four-watts, might increase the number of light fixtures and check if the right wattage light bulbs for the fixtures.

Someone could put tape notes on worn down appliances and other things so a friend will know how to operate them better! People should have two extra sets of keys and mark them for identification for a friend when not at home. People should keep the house key in a HAND before going into the home after unlocking the door, then check to see if the door is properly locked after locking it when inside. Somebody could

use timers to go on and off at different hours for lights and a radio on while nobody is at home.

People should not leave anything on the top of the stove, cooking on the top, or in the oven in case forgetting to turn the oven and stove off, and should have a safety BACKUP PLAN in case there is an electrical power failure! Somebody could turn a six-volt lantern battery upside down into a flashlight so the battery will last longer while not being used for later, which is definitely a very real important considerable thing for some observable over conscious particular people.

Someone could have a round door handle key lock in the front and side doors, two deadbolt key locks each, front door with a small rotating bar with a clip so that it cannot be undone from the outside, and side door with a sliding deadbolt lock with long thick screws! Someone could keep a TOUGH SHIRT on a door hook for a warning, the screened door locked, and the solid door open for a breeze. Somebody might have a vertical sliding chain around the front screened door handle with a small piece of Velcro in the slide so when the chain is up it will not fall down past the Velcro for security, and might put a pair of eyeglasses and something to read near a cup on a folding TV-tray by a chair in view from the door.

People could use aluminum foil so less TOXIC smoke gets on the food when barbecuing, and could use a barbecue scrub pad instead of a wire brush to clean the barbecue grill, because a few small broken wire bristles that look like needles can get on the grill and then on the food which could cause surgery and medical bills. People could wear: protective clothing, eye protection, RESPIRATOR, chemical protection, earplugs, safety hat, gloves, kneepads, or safety shoes so might not get injured while working!

Chapter 2 Safety Helpful Ideas

Shoes should not be tight and RESISTANT to: slipping, floor marking, oil, electrical hazards, abrasions, antimicrobial for odor control, steel protection for toes, and night reflectors if desired? Someone could put a full length green insert into shoes, and cautiously take short slow steps while leaning forward a little when walking on slippery surfaces. Someone should not have SLIPPERY floors and or slippery backing on throw rugs, could attach a throw rug to the floor so it does not move, have a safety hand railing, and might add a caution sign? Somebody might use quick judgment to roll some to dissipate some of the potential energy spread into kinetic energy to lessen an injury if falling down.

Someone could PROTECT themselves when outside in freezing weather with: thermal underwear, warm clothes maybe four layers if needed, facemask, warm hat, snowmobile coat, leather insulated ski mittens or electric gloves, electric socks, insulated boots with 800 grams of insulation, and might put a pair of gloves inside another pair to be warmer, also should salt the outside porch and steps when needed.

Somebody could check the plumbing for REPAIRS, put tape notes on the pipes for what kind of repairs needed, and put an ample amount of silicone-plumbing grease on the required surfaces when doing plumbing repairs. Somebody could put a small amount of plumbing grease on the inside of a plastic shutoff valve hinge, the tangent of the flap to be tested for a closed fit before installing so that it does not leak and stick, and might NEED TO TRIM SOME OF THE EXCESSIVE FLASH MATERIAL IF ANY?

People should read the hot water tank manual to remove some water yearly from the safety release spout and bottom drain until clear water comes out. Someone could drain the hot water tank if less hot water at a cooler temperature

which might indicate having sludge like sediment that needs to come out of the bottom of the tank. Somebody could have an adjustable mirror on a very long handle with a light to examine the back of the hot water tank in a cubbyhole or the undercarriage of a vehicle, and could have a caution sign hanging down to help protect the top of their head from a tight low area by ducking. People should TURN OFF the electric or gas water heater in case no water pressure when going on a vacation so not damaging the two electric heating ELEMENTS.

Someone should replace regular washing machine hoses with NO-BURST stainless steel mesh hoses for better protection, check to see if there is an adequate drain cover by the washing machine, and clean the drain cover if needed. Somebody should check to see if there is an adequate drainage system for flash flood storm water, might drain the water pipes during the winter if going on a vacation so the pipes do not freeze in a mobile home or other structure, and in case a washing machine hose leaks.

Some speeds of trains on curves could be reduced because of the centrifugal changing force $F=MV^2/R$, radial acceleration equals V^2/R, V equals the velocity and R is the radius of the curve. $F=MA$ force equals mass times acceleration effect on the MOTION of the train, and the changing center of gravity effect. Some tracks could be inspected for storm damage after a storm. People that are fantasizing and assuming where usually the devil is are gambling against the world where the environment is! The world is going TOO FAST in some areas and should SLOW DOWN so people could do BETTER work if given MORE TIME to do the work.

Someone could give somebody an early one ring on the phone if going to give him or her a ride in their vehicle so they could start to get ready. Somebody could buy a cushion to put on the damaged driver's seat to dampen bumpy rides a little, put the hazardous flasher lights on, and slow the damaged vehicle down for some potholes. When sitting in a vehicle someone should seal pockets if Velcro, button, or zip them closed so things do NOT slide out, try to keep things in the front trouser pockets instead of the coat pockets, and sew any loose holes closed in pockets so things do not fall out.

A stranger could come to the door holding a large empty box and ask, can you open the door so I can put this box inside, and then Rob the home or Worse! A vehicle might stop where your kids are, the driver could say your mother is injured and offer to give them a ride to their mother, but the kids could ask for TWO SECURITY WORDS. Sterling Heights Public Library DVD j362.88 I AM NOT A TARGET, Lies and Tricks.

The more options in a vehicle the more the vehicle will cost and to repair, and could order a Chassis Repair Manual. Automotive retires can get their spouse, parents, brothers, sons, sisters, daughters, grandchildren, spouse's parents including in-laws and stepchildren discounts on purchased and leased vehicles and other products IF THEY COMMUNICATE. Someone could park the vehicle near where people are walking and or driving so somebody might not turn the outside mirrors, could turn the front wheels all the way right or left when parking in a risky theft area, and could park the vehicle so the DRIVER'S SIDE is facing the home for better visible security.

I should look both ways for the general traffic when washing my car parked close to the sidewalk with two plastic

chairs for protection while staying CLOSE to the car, and the snowplow that usually comes closer when shoveling the snow by the street with my facemask and parka hood on during a dark night of a heavy thick snowfall! I put my wet clothes into the dryer after shoveling the snow and used a warm hair blower to dry myself.

Somebody could lean a hand on a window instead of the painted surface when waxing a classy vehicle, gloss and colors might look different if waxing plastic or rubber exterior grained trim parts. If someone leaves a key in the ignition while working on a vehicle somebody might steal the key, and could have two HIDDEN kill switches installed to a classy vehicle's ignition system for antitheft because of this Unfair Deceptive Cold Stained Busy System of Things!

People could try to keep the area underneath the vehicle's hood DRY so not causing problems of cathode corrosion (metal only), dielectric corrosion (nonmetal), and galvanic corrosion (metal with electricity). I use a long handle floor broom to soft brush some of the dirt off my old rusted car and then hose the loose dirt off. I use a hose, a pail, and a mop to wash my car because old and rusted so not damaging the carwash brushes at an automatic carwash.

Someone should buy the BEST battery, read the BATTERY manual if going to disconnect both cables if not driving the vehicle for more than a month to put the battery in a storage mode so the vehicle should start if the battery was at a full charge, or jump-start the battery if needed. Somebody could have an extra key to use for short distance driving stops and or if a weak battery with the vehicle parked, windows up, doors locked, and engine running so the battery does not get too rundown for next time.

A battery could discharge and become damaged if the top part touches metal, do NOT add any water to a maintenance free battery, could clean the connections, and SECURE the battery to the tray with a tie down bar or other method if needed (wood on four sides if old and rusted like mine). The last trip of driving the vehicle should be for 15 minutes where there is a driving load on the alternator fan while charging the battery.

Kids and pets can DIE if left in a vehicle when sunny and warm! Someone should get a vehicle repaired for SAFETY before it gets worse, and might write a repair paper before driving the vehicle to the write-up service attendant. Someone might ask some questions and review the repairs with the service attendant and the mechanic if needed, look if there are any damages to any ADJACENT parts after the repairs, check the exterior for any damage, look under the hood to see if a shop rag is there, and check if any missing items from the inside of the vehicle and trunk.

I went into the mobile home park office and complained that some of my three old vehicles ornamentation stolen FIVE different times, while somebody else was hearing me they also damaged my vehicles later on, it is usually better to talk on the phone! Someone is usually safer if QUITE and they do not bother anybody. Someone might injure your leg between the car door if open while sitting down, and steal the vehicle if they are close to the door.

People should CHECK before driving if all lights and other things are working, and have the brake lights on as a HABIT if the vehicle is the front or back one stopped, even if no other vehicles are around. Someone could park the vehicle so it will be going forward when going to drive, and could look to see how they have parked the vehicle, each full tire width could be on a flat surface each so not stretching the tire cords.

Somebody might be better off to BACK-UP if going to drive into deep flooded water, or on side street roadwork with wet road construction white cement powder on the road which would be hard to remove! If a vehicle is in deep-flooded water do not start the vehicle, might disconnect the battery cables until dried for a long time, and have the electrical system checked. Somebody could avoid high clumps of frozen ice that are like broken chunks of concrete that might damage a vehicle that is somewhat low to the ground.

Someone could keep a Yellow Pages Phone Book for backup information in a vehicle, read all the new vehicle papers, and test-drive the new vehicle in a safe area. Someone could get a ticket and be INJURED if not stopping when the courteous police officer says stop, might be in a vehicle accident while fantasizing and assuming where usually the devil is, and if trying to get away it will cost more in the end when caught.

People could make a help sign, SEND HELP for their vehicle and home in case needed. People should avoid driving into pedestrians and other vehicles if going to get into an accident involving an animal. People should pay visual ATTENTION to the forward direction while driving slow on a residential street for pedestrians such as a woman with white short shorts, regular traffic, vehicles that are running stop signs, and stray animals!

People should slow the vehicle down and increase the following distance when the roads are wet, slippery, or in a thunderstorm, and could stay off the roads sometime if snow

and ice are on the roads, it is better to be safe than sorry! People should use the turn signal sooner and LOOK at the rearview mirror, because some vehicles are too close and traveling at faster speeds than the limit, if so keep going further, and make the turn ahead.

More people are usually in a weekend or a holiday than during a regular weekday as intoxicated drivers on alcohol and or drugs while fantasizing and assuming where usually the devil is. People should turn off the road safely if driving when a drunk driver's vehicle is driving towards while crossing the center of the road side-to-side to let it pass, or face a possible head-on collision with expensive MEDICAL BILLS because of this Unfair Deceptive Cold Stained Busy System of Things!

Someone that is fantasizing and assuming where usually the devil is while rushing will lose accuracy and quality of some things now and then, and should REDUCE the distractions in a vehicle to be more observant of important driving conditions! Someone cannot see the traffic in the next lane and somebody waves to come on, do NOT do it, should wait to SEE to go a safe way if wanting to drive perpendicular through open stopped traffic!

People could reduce the probability of getting into a vehicle accident by going to more than one place at a driving time, and might slow the vehicle down SAFELY to let an oncoming vehicle on the expressway when driving in the right lane. People could get a ticket and be injured if not stopping for a yellow light, and should play it safe if a vehicle is following close while approaching a yellow light.

Someone in a vehicle accident should call the POLICE to get the accident reported for safety, medical, and financial

reasons. Someone could write the other Vehicle's Identification Number from the outside at the driver's side by the front window, from the top of the dashboard, or copy their Vehicle Identification Number from the Certificate of No-Fault Insurance or Registration, and get their Driver's License and Plate Numbers!

People do not know how fast a vehicle is moving or how close it is from the front view, and should WAIT until the oncoming traffic clears both ways if going to make a turn onto a two-way double lanes roadway! Someone might be able to go to a side street or a traffic light where it might be safer, look both ways TWICE for any traffic, and then enter safely to a visible cleared lane.

People should not drive close to parked vehicles when driving in a parking lot because one of the parked ones might be backing out without the driver looking enough. People should put the hazardous flasher warning lights on when driving slow in a tight parking lot, and when LOOKING at the mirrors and windows while backing out VERY SLOW of a parking space! Somebody could step behind the vehicle just after looking at the mirrors, be driving by, backing theirs out the same time behind yours, or from a close parking space.

Vehicles should not be too close to the light because a LONG large truck might need to make a wide turn, people should LOOK at the nearby traffic before starting on the green light and when making a turn, because large vehicles and other ones are running red lights now and then! A vehicle's turn signal is used to change lanes so the turn signal should be on sooner and look TWICE to see if it is clear, and use the turn signal sooner to change to one lane at a time because another quiet vehicle might be changing to the same lane at the same time (Left arm and hand bent up for a RIGHT turn, left arm and hand straight out for a LEFT turn, left arm and hand bent down for slow or stop)!

Someone could put the heater switch on high and the AIR CONDITIONING on to decrease the humidity if the inside side of the windows starts to get FOGGY. Someone should not speedup if following close to a vehicle in front while approaching a green light, because the light could turn yellow with the front vehicle suddenly stopping, and could flicker the bright lights to caution a vehicle that is close while thinking it might turn in front of yours.

My car stopped at a traffic light seventh car back waiting for the traffic to go with my lights on, foot on the break peddle, seatbelt and sunglasses on, and using the sun visor by the front windshield. A car going about 25 miles per hour on a very sunny day rear-ended my car. I got ONLY $500 FOR THE REPAIRS from the nephew's owner! Somebody could mail a copy of the police report to the owner's insurance company, and an expensive court case could be required if in a large claim of auto and medical. People should stay away from dangerous driving conditions, unfavorable people, dangerous sports, and anything else with RISKY movements!

I parked my car back in the designated area so another vehicle might not back-up against the bumper, but would have been better off to park somewhere else, because a truck backed to my car, hooked the end of the front bumper, and SEVERELY DAMAGED THE BUMPER! The truck that damaged my car was gone and there were no witnesses! Small companies as well as all others should have designated parking for construction vehicles and other different kinds of long vehicles! People could park in a safer parking space such as the inside perimeter of a parking lot, further away from other vehicles, by the sidewalk, or by a security camera.

Chapter 2 Safety Helpful Ideas

People could go to the BUYER'S BANK when selling a used vehicle to get a certified check, go to a Sectary of State Branch Office to transfer the title, and have the vehicle taken off the insurance policy after signing the title off. The Sectary of State Branch Offices could have some vehicles checked for safety when getting annual License Plate Tabs. People should get a 90-page book of *What Every Driver Must Know* from a Sectary of State Branch Office to study the book, and a safe driving course book to mark the multiple choice test question answers every three years to become safer drivers while reducing their auto insurance cost! People should watch safe driving DVDS from the library to help avoid from getting into an accident. People that do not read and study *What Every Driver Must Know* and do not study a safe driving course book are usually dangerous drivers in this Unfair Deceptive Cold Stained Busy System of Things which is: NOT GETTING GOOD information, advice, EDUCATION, mentoring, counseling, tutoring, or follow-up EARLY IN LIFE and later on, being uninformed, DECEPTION, greed, verbal and physical abuse, LACK OF BETTER EDUCATION, COMMUNICATIONS, religion, ethics, time, money, and love!

Everybody can profit from the variety of the diversification of some of these many HELPFUL IDEAS, some more, some less depending on their experiences in life. You could do this, should do that, or you might do something else different, good luck.

Chapter 2 Safety Helpful Ideas

Chapter 3 Health Helpful Ideas

PEOPLE SHOULD CHECK WITH QUALIFIED ORGANIZATIONS WITH THEIR PEOPLE FOR ADVICE.

I use capitalization and or underlining to emphasize throughout my book. Everybody has different experiences in life from what mentoring, counseling, tutoring, advice, information, and follow-up they got at an early age IF ANY in this UNFAIR DECEPTIVE COLD STAINED BUSY SYSTEM OF THINGS which is: NOT GETTING GOOD information, advice, EDUCATION, mentoring, counseling, tutoring, or follow-up EARLY IN LIFE and later on, being uninformed, DECEPTION, greed, verbal and physical abuse, LACK OF BETTER EDUCATION, COMMUNICATIONS, religion, ethics, time, money, and love! THE SCHOOLS COULD HAVE A MENTORING COURSE AT AN EARLY AGE TO IMPROVE the system AND BE MENTORED EARLY and in the SENIOR YEAR!

I buy multi-grain cinnamon swirl raisin bread and separate the slices before freezing, cake, vegan pie, and cookies, put them into the freezer, and later take the cake, pie, cookies, or bread out to eat while watching a colorful ultrahigh definition television which is not that hard to do. I eat some SMALL meals sometime of same like kinds of foods and large meals of different foods, use a strong fork with a thick handle and a folded kitchen washcloth for added comfort to remove low fat frozen yogurt from a three-gallon container, and later take a long siesta after eating which is also not that hard to do.

I bought a LARGE size sold leather belt so that it does not come apart, sometime wear suspenders instead of a belt so

might help my posture, rarely wear some clothes inside out against my skin for smoother comfort, and not tight. I wear a hat outside usually when the weather with the wind-chill factor is less than 70° F because (I am a baby) do not want to get sick. I use a heavy decorative glass fruit bowl as a pedestal to put a soup or cereal bowl onto to raise them above the table so do not have to bend down AS FAR, which is definitely a very real big important substantial delightful considerable thing for some distinguished people.

Do NOT lick any food container surfaces because of toxins. I try to stay healthy and strong while thinking of how to IMPROVE my health, and eat an energy food such as: a rich trail mix, if my granola cereal is too hard to chew I break it down with a hammer outside of the bag, dried fruit, fruitcake, vegan pie, cookies, frozen sweet desert strawberries, baklava, or organic dates an hour before doing strenuous exercise or manual labor. I should not eat right before doing manual labor because of feeling full after eating and so more blood can go to my muscles instead of going to the digestive system, and rest for a day before an event.

I buy some fresh produce, cook some food until hot before cautiously eating, recook cold food that is starting to get old to help PROTECT from bacteria and medical bills, then try NOT to eat expired food so not getting sick. I usually eat sweet ripe fruit instead of unripe fruit, warm sweet food instead of cold bitter food. I drink cold ice water with fresh lemon juice and maple syrup from my cup that was in the freezer, organic apple juice in a gallon glass container instead of pop, organic coconut milk, fat free milk Lactose free 0% milk fat. I eat Lactose free ice-cream, not some kinds of fruit with some kinds of vegetables, clean some fruit and vegetables with Vegetable and Fruit Wash and eat some of them raw because microwaving and cooking destroys some of the good enzymes.

Chapter 3 Health Helpful Ideas

I buy only enough food so the food might not spoil, have a THERMOS BOTTLE (not a cup because colder and less dust) to drink cold filtered water from a Zero Water Filter System each day and some water is already in foods. Cottage cheese with sliced peaches, cold stewed tomatoes, sweet pineapple in cans, and sweet cherries in jars all make handy snacks. Thai King chicken rice soup, fried rice with chicken or beef are healthy to eat while helping to decrease weight. I eat better food, get better rest, and do different exercise to IMPROVE my health.

I am allergic to some tree, grass, weed, and flower pollens, eat organic dates, drink tea with honey and lemon, buy organic foods like large raisins, fresh dates, figs, multi-grain enriched flower, and organic virgin light coconut oil for cooking. I REDUCE WEIGHT by reducing sweets, bakery, dairy products, salt, white flower, white sugar, and butter, and sometime replace salt with Bragg's Liquid Amino all-purpose seasoning in a spray bottle that is vegetable protein from soybeans and purified water.

I buy better nonorganic and organic foods because some of todays' foods have less nourishment causing me to eat more while becoming overweight. I get better produce than the less expensive, put DATES on tape of a few glass container lids of a few foods, and put them into the refrigerator set at 34° F. I double wrap some foods so staying fresher longer in the refrigerator and freezer, and do not put some particular tropical types of fruit into the refrigerator such as mangos and plums because the cold temperature will turn them brown.

I have some liquids first or soft food and end with harder dry foods. I try NOT to drink liquids while eating solids, because the digestive juices will not be able to digest the food properly. I stay upright for a while after eating so some

food might not back-up, and might drink TWO cups of warm filtered water if getting sick to dilute some of the toxins. I might drink two warm cups of water if vomited the food to dilute some of the remaining toxins and vomit some of that up as a rinse of some of the leftover toxins.

I CAUTIOUSLY and slowly massage my skin with a 10-inch paddle brush with 100 molded ends and or an 18-inch shower brush with 1,800 soft bristles to vitalize my tender skin. I read a thick medical book about the human body, and a nutritional health-healing book chapter about Food Grade 35 Percent Hydrogen Peroxide from a health store which is bitter but good for you.

I lose some weight until at the recommended weight with the FAMILY DOCTOR'S approval by eating one meal, one snack an apple and or orange, and drinking filtered water daily when hungry, and exercise is beneficial but usually contributes to a small amount of weight loss. I check my weight and waistline measurement at two spots plotted on graph paper monthly and write the things that are affecting them.

I gain strength by: deep sleeping from a good social home environment, (live alone) time of day, IMPROVED body condition, snug clothes, could put a rubber-band around pajama cuffs to be warmer, dim lights, noise to a minimum, comfortable temperature and humidity, firm bed, one small soft thin pillow (Meijer) for sleeping on my back then fold in half for twice the thickness to sleep on sides if desired, and large flannel sheet, and blanket.

I bend to the left with the right arm overhead while stretching the right side a little because of a medical letter. I do calf raises every third day or so by standing on a wood board

16 inches long by 6 inches wide by 2 inches thick near a table, do calf raises a different way to work the NEGLECTED calf muscle by leaning forward to support on my forearms on a table, and sometime after massage calf muscles cautiously so they might not seize up later at night while in bed. Do NOT over strain yourself or could cause you to lose some of your strength which could take a very long time for a pulled muscle or tendon with old injuries at an older age to partially heal, the healing is notoriously slow (just do not touch it), and a blue icepack should be in an enclosed cloth jacket so not touching the skin for 5 minutes.

I use rubber exercise stretch tubing to do exercise CAUTIOUSLY within reason after checking with the FAMILY DOCTOR. I do a few squats for legs while standing on a wood board near a couch or chair. I tighten or flex my old injured right external oblique stomach muscle injury from scanning groceries while getting into bed so there is less pain. I stand by the bed while trying to keep balanced when getting dressed and undressed to help strengthen legs and midsection by using legs to get up from sitting and down from standing, not arms.

I bought a firm packaged spongy cushion ring from a Medical Equipment and Supply Store for sitting on hard surfaces because of a MEDICAL LETTER, used the cushion ring at a high school graduation sitting on a metal chair, at a store on a plastic chair while eating, at an amusement park at a wood picnic table outside while eating, and while reading by a swimming pool sitting on a plastic chair.

Once in a long time I lay on my stomach on the bed and push up on my hands to arch up backwards. I relax my knees sometime on the edge of the mattress while cautiously stretching my back leg muscles and hamstrings, or while

sitting on a chair put my heels up on another chair with no shoes on. I do partial side roll sit-ups once in a while by laying on my back on the carpet with a small soft pillow for my head to help straighten my back, and once RESTED to get some of my strength back because of being weak from the flu.

A warm SHOWER, moist HEATING PAD, warm HAIR BLOWER, and an ELECTRIC MASSAGER can reduce pain if done right, and a thin COLD PACK in a towel jacket for 5 minutes can reduce heat and inflammation. I have some aches and pains that are not use to when doing different manual movements, could continue to have back pain if continuing to stretch lumbar muscles, and might rest aches and pains for a week or go to a DOCTOR.

I do a few hand exercises with a two-and-a-half-inch diameter firm rubber ball to strengthen hands and FINGERS, by squeezing the ball in a hand and then just between two fingers at a time while having one heel on the couch with no shoes on, then the other leg the same way. I use a Thera Wall Body Massager (1-800-548-4097) with seven massaging rollers on a cord to reduce pain by targeting key pressure areas that are hard to reach, back, shoulders, legs, arms, and once in a long time I use an electric massager.

I breathe through my nose when outside to filter the air inhaled for a healthier condition, and might do ONE deep inhaling breathe cautiously once a week to help keep lungs at near capacity. The one deep inhaling breath might increase the inside and outside size of my chest a very small amount? I use Ocean Saline Nasal Spray for nasal membranes, chlorine free soft Kleenex, and organic cotton Q-tips.

Chapter 3 Health Helpful Ideas

I could damage my eyes if looking at the sun so do NOT look at the sun, and after checking with an EYE DOCTOR might cautiously do a few eye exercises of different movements to strengthen my eye muscles. I use current two pair of eyeglass frames and sunglass frames for three new pair of eyeglasses if in good condition, and use Dawn Liquid Soap to clean the frames.

I wipe my eyelashes with a washcloth and get very small thin threads on them, check with an EYE DOCTOR before removing an eyelash off an eye with cold filtered water in a small paper cup or just wait so gravity might work it out, and use Advanced Visine. I use a regular small flashlight, not a LED (light-emitting diode) flashlight to see while CAUTIOUSLY removing a loose eyelash and a few small particles from my eyelashes with a clean small fingernail or a small clean mascara wand.

I should NOT scratch my skin or rub eyelids while working outside with fingers because might plant bacteria or fungi into the surface of my tender skin, and wash hands with a good soap as soon as going back inside after working outside. I remove a very small hair that is tickling by the side of my nose by using a magnifying glass, flashlight, and tweezers.

I brush my teeth with pea size toothpaste on the top surface, on gums with a small circular motion, and then pull up towards the top of teeth to help prevent from getting recessed gums so might not have to get an expensive root canal, or the problem might be a mild sensitive nerve. I get a Dental Florid Varnish Treatment and use Colgate Sensitive Mild Mint Toothpaste on sensitive teeth. I use Glide Dental Floss by tying the ends of one foot of dental floss in a CIRCLE with four knots together, move the floss to the adjacent tooth while CURVING, forcefully drawing mouthwash between teeth after dental

flossing, and try to keep wisdom teeth, tonsils, and adenoids as part of my whole body immune system.

I clean some body utensils in a plastic cup with 70 percent Isopropyl Rubbing Alcohol, then combs, brush, and anything else that touches my skin with Dawn Liquid Soap. I brush my teeth in the morning, eat a warm sweet cereal, and brush teeth before going to the dentist. Dental X-rays every 6 months for 75 years are 150 X-rays to see if there are any problems. I reduce some X-rays and other test by signing a paper, but I first REVIEW if might want to change my mind.

Colonic Hydrotherapy Treatments at a Healing Arts Center can clean my large intestine some, Chiropractic adjustments and an electric massager can reduce pain while IMPROVING my posture and health. Pressure Point Therapy done by a physical therapist very cautiously can decrease pain, but I first check with my FAMILY DOCTOR.

I could bring a magnifying glass and a mirror if the dermatologist says, that hard to see spot that itch every day for the past two years from an old insect sting does not have to be treated (or it might be a fungus scalp humidity infection)? A DERMATOLOGIST can remove warts with liquid nitrogen on a long Q-tip, and IMPROVE other skin needs. I put chemicals on my skin and some of them are absorbed into the skin, and they could go to other internal areas of my body.

I first check with a DERMATOLOGIST to use antifungal or antibacterial cream, Zeasorb Powder, or a light lotion Vanicream. Zeasorb Powder is a powder that absorbs THREE times more moisture than plain talcum powder from the pharmacy for skin rashes, itchy skin, and electric shaving

if desired with a regular small flashlight to see for shaving, not a LED (light-emitting diode) flashlight.

I cautiously massage my skin from head to toes to vitalize my tender skin, and rub off an old top layer of skin from some areas of my body. I massage an area of my body CAUTIOUSLY that aches with fingers or with a dry coarse towel, and use a small portable massage lounge mat with low and high settings for massage and heat. I write a paper with medical information before going to the friendly family doctor to get a medical letter for a condition. Females could go to FEMALE DOCTORS if open to save some money instead of an emergency center at a hospital for minor care and a referral doctor's phone number.

I am cautious of what is said to doctors and other people when in buildings as well as outside because of ethics, verbal abuse, tape recorders, inside and outside cameras, and SECURITY people! I do not go to the doctor when having minor aches and pains while not knowing what part of my body needs attention if ingesting pain pills, or might DIE from surgery and drugs. Some doctors say heart medicine is like candy and can get the Blood Pressure reading down to 115, while some medical personnel check the pressure manually and say it is 140. Some doctors say when the blood pressure gets to 140 go to an emergency center for an EVALUATION. I sometime check the reading at home in the morning with a ReliOn Automatic Blood Pressure Monitor when not doing manual labor, rested for one day, and alone while doing a math problem mentally.

Someone that smokes tobacco contributes to the thinning of their hair, because the smoke can damage some of their healthy hair follicle glands, they could detox, do exercise, and meditate. People could stay away from some toxins, go to

a FAMILY DOCTOR, DETOX, have a not alcoholic beverage such as spicy Bloody Marry Mix to sip slowly, cold juice, sweet apple cider, or zero calorie ginger ale with a fizz.

People that take in tobacco, alcohol, drugs, wasteful gambling, illicit sex, and reckless things will suffer! People that drink alcohol and eat toxins while fantasizing and assuming where usually the devil is are contributing to the destruction of their appendix, kidneys, gallbladder, liver, and BRAIN CELLS that do not heal because they are not muscles. Their systems might chemically start to gradually shutdown if they become rancid, form stones, skin turns yellowish, or their food tastes like chemicals, because the liver does not remove some of them and when it fills up it shouts DOWN! People could get exercise literature and diagrams from the physiatrist and physical therapist, DVDS from the LIBRARY, and could do easy warm-up exercises every third day or so, if not might have to get a cane, handrail walker, wheelchair, or be bedridden in this Unfair Deceptive Cold Stained Busy System of Things which is: NOT GETTING GOOD information, advice, EDUCATION, mentoring, counseling, tutoring, or follow-up EARLY IN LIFE and later on, being uninformed, DECEPTION, greed, verbal and physical abuse, LACK OF BETTER EDUCATION, COMMUNICATIONS, religion, ethics, time, money, and love!

Everybody can profit from the variety of the diversification of some of these many HELPFUL IDEAS, some more, some less depending on their experiences in life. You could do this, should do that, or you might do something else different, good luck.

Chapter 4 Family Helpful Ideas

PEOPLE SHOULD CHECK WITH QUALIFIED ORGANIZATIONS WITH THEIR PEOPLE FOR ADVICE.

I use capitalization and or underlining to emphasize throughout my book. Everybody has different experiences in life from what mentoring, counseling, tutoring, advice, information, and follow-up they got at an early age IF ANY in this UNFAIR DECEPTIVE COLD STAINED BUSY SYSTEM OF THINGS which is: NOT GETTING GOOD information, advice, EDUCATION, mentoring, counseling, tutoring, or follow-up EARLY IN LIFE and later on, being uninformed, DECEPTION, greed, verbal and physical abuse, LACK OF BETTER EDUCATION, COMMUNICATIONS, religion, ethics, time, money, and love! THE SCHOOLS COULD HAVE A <u>MENTORING COURSE</u> AT AN EARLY AGE TO <u>IMPROVE</u> the system AND BE <u>MENTORED EARLY</u> and in the <u>SENIOR YEAR</u>!

People that want to have a BETTER relationship with their spouse could sit with their spouse on a love couch while holding their hand and saying nice things, do a few favors for her or him while building points up, and when accumulated enough points their spouse might unload them by doing nice things for them. Someone will then have to start over, cutting the grass does not count but will still have to cut the grass before it rains and wear protective clothing, and sometime somebody could cut only the front lawn by the street if the back lawn is not growing as much as the front lawn.

Chapter 4 Family Helpful Ideas

People could phone friends to wish them a Happy New-Year and for advice, they could save some New Year's Eve colorful party hats and other things for a future party. People could write NAMES AND PHONE NUMBERS of some older religious educated people that meet for later for advice. Somebody might buy a fashionable shoe bag to put dance shoes into when going to a dance to meet another dancer, and do not worry hors d'oeuvres will probably be there.

People should have a better chance in the world if living in the educational state of mind that is the educational material from the schools and libraries, and the spiritual state of mind that is good Bible STUDIES with their parents early in life for five years and then longer, and in the schools. People could listen to a few religious radio and TV channels for spiritual meditation, betterment, music to relax by, have weekly FAMILY MEETINGS, EDUCATIONAL material from the friendly library, decent educational games like Dominoes and Scrabble, and do-good Bible STUDIES like in a class with their family.

People will probably be all right if going straight by the Bible within reason, but IF going against the Bible while fantasizing and assuming where usually the devil is will have problems such as a divorce. People not communicating with their parents and spouse will NOT benefit, and the easiest way of doing things is not always the best way for them. Someone might lose employment if talking about divorce problems at work, and a couple can get a divorce for less than $100 IF the conditions are right and they do the paperwork.

Chapter 4 Family Helpful Ideas

People that do not work for things and get them free do not appreciate or take care of them as much as if they have worked for them. Some people could work THREE days a week for some professions, do-good Bible STUDIES with their family THREE days a week, and have weekly family meetings. People could write who, what, how, where, when, why, and FAMILY APPROVAL for decision-making if having the time to do that, and learn better by listening, NOT by talking. People usually do not do things right the first time and usually do not get a second chance, but that is one way we all lose and learn.

News on the radio and television is deceptive some or Worse. People could review questions written on paper before making a phone call, just because somebody says something does not mean that the information is true, could be a lie, forged, or only ONE sided, and could ask for verified documentation! Most of the mentally ill people are not really mentally ill, they just have NOT been mentored better in the SCHOOLS in this Unfair Deceptive Cold Stained Busy System of Things!

What the kids and children are watching on a colorful ultrahigh definition television, who they are associating with, what they see, hear, and do will affect their personalities. Somebody that has kids and children and brings a colorful ultrahigh definition television with the Internet computer into their bedrooms might corrupt them, waste their time, and work against them and you. Home personal computers connected to the Internet have drawbacks of some people playing games too much, X-rated material leading to some pregnancies, and some school dropouts, or might go to the library to get EDUCATED.

Chapter 4 Family Helpful Ideas

Someone could have a colorful ultrahigh definition television in the front room, and a computer not connected to the Internet for children to do their accounting school assignments in the basement. Someone might add one or two holes to a recessed television enclosure, add a small fan if needed to REDUCE heat, and have an electrical surge protector with a built-in charger.

Parents should have physical contact with their kids, children, and family of handshakes, hugs, kisses, and back-to-back hand-to-hand pulls to DECREASE STRESS within reason, or somebody else will unjustly do it. A daughter might get pregnant and or not finish school if dressing her as a fashion model with skimpy clothes and makeup on because of some fashioned advertisements and fantasy movies. If giving the kids most of everything they will not have to do as much other than watching television, eating, sleeping, and going to the bathroom.

There is not enough time in a day to do the things in a marriage which contributes to DIVORCES, and might become an achiever in life if your spouse complements you, amen. Women behind successful men might also become successful, men ahead of unsuccessful women might also become unsuccessful, marriages will suffer if giving too much to everybody else, and if telling the people at work that you are going to get married they might ruin your marriage and also become divorced like me. You usually can accomplish more if single and live alone in a small home, amen.

People lose CONTROL if giving the kids or pets dominance, and when walking their dog with a proper choker harness up at the front of the upper neck, behind the ears and head as a show dog for more control will not experience the dog pulling as much as at the lower thicker part of the neck.

Chapter 4 Family Helpful Ideas

The Humane Society will euthanize a few pets so give somebody the innocent pet free if not being able to take care of the pet.

Somebody took an attractive high school senior girl's heavy set of keys from a small table while she was facing the other way on a lounge chair with a tiny bikini on. She had earphones on while sun tanning at the mobile home park pool with cool dark sunglasses while snapping her fingers to the music. An adult stranger from behind in a deep macho voice asked if he could have a CIGARETTE from the table, she never looked at the person and said OK, she could have taken only one key and protected the key to get back into her home!

People could wait for somebody equal to so there is less arguments, because they have only ONE FIRST CHANCE of being happily married but the odds are strongly against them, and could try to marry a relative or someone that like with a college degree in the same academic area and or workplace of interest. People might be better to stay lively single and in school in this unfair changing world as long as can.

People might not get good information, advice, counseling, mentoring, tutoring, and follow-up early in life from older people, should have THREE mentors, and communicate effectively, if not then NOT benefiting. People could make a plus and minus sheet, fishbone diagram, or a flowchart of what the results might be in the future.

Husband and spouse submit to the Christ, spouse submits to the husband, children submit to the parents and can get advice from the church. Someone could try to stay neutral with people, not swear and force them to do something they do not want to do, and should not criticize and embarrass

someone in the presence of others, unless it is for a very good reason. Women are moody, men are more stable, and it just takes only ONE thing to ruin a marriage.

People that tease their innocent spouse about other people might cause their spouse to do the same to them because of curiosity, and that might lead to consequences that could be serious. Nobody is going to do anything for you unless they want to do it, half to do it, or paid to do so, and some people that you meet will use and abuse you to get what they can then leave you to SUFFER. If you are fantasizing and assuming you are usually gambling with the devil, and if you do not communicate with your parents and spouse you do NOT benefit.

Verbal abuse can be just as bad as physical abuse, and if not knowing what to do and say do NOT do or say anything, unless it is helpful! There is a SOCIAL REACTION NOW OR IN THE FUTURE FOR EVERY SOCIAL ACTION and it is about being uninformed, DECEPTION, greed, verbal and physical abuse, LACK OF BETTER EDUCATION, COMMUNICATIONS, religion, ethics, time, money, and love because of this Unfair Deceptive Cold Stained Busy System of Things!

You could blend down with people, say that have less than what they have, if different might change, or might move to a different environment and get MORE EDUCATION. Some rich people that do not have to work for a living have a better chance of staying married, or they could stay lively single, do-good Bible STUDIES, try to stay in the schools, join social clubs, and have real estate and toys.

Chapter 4 Family Helpful Ideas

People could write the reasons why they would want to get married while fantasizing and assuming, and for why would want to stay lively single while thinking about the world where the ENVIRONMENT IS! People that want to get married could: do-good Bible STUDIES with their parents early in life for five years and then longer, and in the schools, learn to read a better way with a study skills course, write a better way, study an ANGER MANAGEMENT COURSE, get mentored, earn a college degree of interest, wait for somebody equal to so there is less arguments, and become TWENTY-EIGHT years of age when the brain is mostly developed. People could try to marry someone from a family where the parents and children are college educated and christens that are NOT pretenders.

A spouse can file for a divorce while fantasizing and assuming where usually the devil is with false pretense anytime! A spouse can drag their husband through the court system with seven attorneys for five years that take what both worked for 20 years, because of this Unfair Deceptive Cold Stained Busy System of Things of not getting mentored, and a human sparked inadvertent computer ERROR from Fidelity Brokerage Services W362135-30NOV17. Some people with physical and mental injuries do not want to get married or stay married.

People should NOT exaggerate when giving information and saying answers, if so they should update the information and answers when available. People should not talk about their: self, brag, physique, height, weight, age, disabilities, sexual orientation, race, color, ancestry, religion, marital status, political beliefs, or source of payments. People should not tell or show something to someone so the information could be safer, and if telling somebody that tells another more information than is required within reason might tell somebody along the way and then they will probably find out about the confidential information.

I usually lose right away if doing one thing wrong, when doing right scarcely NOBODY will say anything for years as if do not exist. I usually learn better by experiencing and reading than watching and listening to somebody that is entertaining dishonestly! I usually try to do five POSITIVE noticeable things each day, review the positive things when in bed to help to fall asleep, and stay in bed longer if tired which is not that hard to do.

Somebody is sort of a new employee to the company and might ask the second new supervisor WHY if that supervisor says change the already approved piece cost figure of their part (robots are not DECEPTIVE but expensive). Somebody might ask for information, advice, mentoring, counseling, tutoring, and follow-up like their Dad would give, but that usually does not happen, or right on the spot during life. They might change the figure anyway if still do not agree, or get a different job, MORE EDUCATION, and some people are brain washed to destroy somebody instead of helping them.

Somebody might do something wrong at work if their spouse puts them down at home and lose employment that day, or stay lively single, amen. A supervisor ignores somebody at work and does not want to be bothered if they have a question. A different supplier brags for a half-hour near somebody prior to lunch, then their supplier takes them out to lunch and brags of sexual abuse during lunch that day because of alcohol, the world is getting more socially toxic and POLLUTED each year! Somebody might be better off to take a sick day or go to a very small island, live there with a nice new friend, eat nice organic sweet ripe bananas, coconuts, pineapples, and surely live their happily ever after with the new nice friend, amen.

Chapter 4 Family Helpful Ideas

Religions that have different beliefs than the Bible could cause some problems, and if you want to become HAPPY become a Jehovah's Witness. People could DO-GOOD Bible STUDIES with the Jehovah's Witnesses of reading four pages and underlining 20 to 30 question answers in the reading per week from an early age with their parents for spiritual meditation. People could do sign language gestures to keep things low-keyed when the next-door neighbors do not speak the same language, and as part of a security system might let the next-door neighbor's kids play on the lawn within reason, and could have two outside chairs at the front of the home.

People with a college degree can usually communicate better with another person with a college degree than a 9th grader. Some people could learn behaviors and the essentials of life an IMPROVED way by saying pardon me, excuse me, you are welcome, please, thank you, and earn a better education. People that are having social and other problems should get them resolved as SOON as can, and will lose positions in some areas because life is competitive with technological changes, so CONTINUE to get educated, have proper experiences, and strengthen current areas.

Verbal abuse can be just as bad as physical abuse, and if not knowing what to do and say do NOT do or say anything, unless it is helpful! People that are not religious, mentored, or educated well usually cannot reason well, use verbal abuse, and sometime even sucker punch if not mentored better and then should take an ANGER MANAGEMENT COURSE. Newton's Law of Action, basically for every action there is a reaction, and for EVERY SOCIAL ACTION THERE IS A SOCIAL REACTION NOW AND OR IN THE FUTURE!

Somebody could have an ugly tree branch to scare their kids if they are not behaving, or check with the library. Actors in movies are not really hit it just looks that way because of cutting and editing of the film. The love relationship will be OVER if your spouse hits you, just like a divorce because the love that is in the heart is HARMED and the brain does NOT forget! People should be given an opportunity when applying for a divorce to study an ANGER MANAGEMENT COURSE, we are living in a very UNFAIR deceptive world!

People should have a better chance in the world if living in the educational state of mind that is the EDUCATIONAL material from the schools and libraries, and the spiritual state of mind that is good Bible STUDIES with their parents early in life for five years and then longer, and in the schools. People should not hit anybody because people are God's CREATION, there should be better religion and love in the world not DECEPTION, sins, and violence, but the world is being socially polluted more each year and is going the WRONG WAY. People that are fantasizing and assuming where usually the devil is are gambling against the world ENVIRONMENT in this Unfair Deceptive Cold Stained Busy System of Things!

People could review things in the home to see which things to IMPROVE, organize, add, remove, and find any forgotten items. People could try to do things ahead of time (ride the wave on the top instead of at the bottom) if having the time and money to do that. People usually cause most of their problems, and could try to prevent a problem like a divorce by trying to correct the causes of the problem.

People could have a three-by-five card with a HEALTHY grocery list in ink on both sides, and another with none grocery items, erase the pencil plus signs for the items not wanted for next time, remove and add items, and mark a plus sign by the items needed. People could decrease the moisture control in the refrigerator, freezer, and furnace during

weather months that are less humid, increase the moisture control during weather months that are more humid, and set the furnace humidity at 50 percent or so.

People might not get proper service and all the items ordered for a meal if giving the new waiter the tip before getting the food, and having to call the waiter back four times when they can find that waiter? People could CHECK all the carryout items they are supposed to get if they are there, usually get service when speaking-up but if not saying anything just vegetate, and could mark a carryout menu for the items might want for next time. Waitress could write the additional things wanted on the op right side of the bill.

The world has problems because people are NOT MENTORED A BETTER WAY AND THEREFORE DO NOT COMMUNICATE EFFECTIVELY CAUSING HUMAN ERRORS AND MISTAKES, there must be something WRONG with this Unfair Deceptive Cold Stained Busy System of Things, SCHOOL SYSTEMS, DIVORCE LAWS, MARRIAGE COUNSELORS, religious organizations, and fashioned spouses!

Marriage is like getting a very complicated package that knowing only a very little about and there are NO DIRECTIONS with the package unless having the time and money to be mentored, counseled, tutored, advised, and informed with follow-up. Marriage should be about love, not verbal and physical abuse. People that get the last verbal abuse word in might cause the other person to get even either now and or in the future, verbal abuse can be just as bad as physical abuse, and if not knowing what to do and say do NOT do or say anything, unless it is helpful! THERE IS A SOCIAL REACTION NOW AND OR IN THE FUTURE FOR EVERY SOCIAL ACTION! THE SCHOOLS COULD HAVE A

MENTORING COURSE AT AN EARLY AGE TO IMPROVE the system AND BE MENTORED EARLY and in the SENIOR YEAR! There could be a RADIO and TV CHANNEL about marriage because marriage counselors usually do NOT help!

I went to TWELVE different kinds of sort of marriage counselors and NOBODY did anything constructive for me about my marriage as if do NOT exist, and TWELVE out of THIRTEEN relationships in my family ended in divorces presently! If you do not want to get divorced do not get married. People are usually brain washed to destroy somebody instead of helping them. People that want to get married could: do-good Bible STUDIES with their parents early in life for five years and then longer, and in the schools, learn to read a better way with a study skills course, write a better way, study an ANGER MANAGEMENT COURSE, get MENTORED, earn a college degree of interest, WAIT for somebody equal to so there is less arguments, and become TWENTY-EIGHT years of age when the brain is mostly developed. Wording of sticks and stones will break my bones but names will never hurt me should be DELETED from all statements! People could use psychology to setup some artificial barriers to help protect from other people in this Unfair Deceptive Cold Stained Busy System of Things which is: NOT GETTING GOOD information, EDUCATION, advice, mentoring, counseling, tutoring, or follow-up EARLY IN LIFE and later on, being uninformed, DECEPTION, greed, verbal and physical abuse, LACK OF BETTER EDUCATION, COMMUNICATIONS, religion, ethics, time, money, and love!

Chapter 4 Family Helpful Ideas

Everybody can profit from the variety of the diversification of some of these many HELPFUL IDEAS, some more, some less depending on their experiences in life. You could do this, should do that, or you might do something else different, good luck.

Chapter 4 Family Helpful Ideas

Chapter 5 Other Helpful Ideas

PEOPLE SHOULD CHECK WITH QUALIFIED ORGANIZATIONS WITH THEIR PEOPLE FOR ADVICE.

I use capitalization and or underlining to emphasize throughout my book. Everybody has different experiences in life from what mentoring, counseling, tutoring, advice, information, and follow-up they got at an early age IF ANY in this UNFAIR DECEPTIVE COLD STAINED BUSY SYSTEM OF THINGS which is: NOT GETTING GOOD information, advice, EDUCATION, mentoring, counseling, tutoring, or follow-up EARLY IN LIFE and later on, being uninformed, DECEPTION, greed, verbal and physical abuse, LACK OF BETTER EDUCATION, COMMUNICATIONS, religion, ethics, time, money, and love! THE SCHOOLS COULD HAVE A <u>MENTORING COURSE</u> AT AN EARLY AGE TO <u>IMPROVE</u> the system AND BE <u>MENTORED EARLY</u> and in the <u>SENIOR YEAR</u>!

People should have the phone numbers of two close people, and HOURS of two close stores for food and other items in case repairing a vehicle and having to walk to one of those stores during the cold windy freezing weather. Somebody might put something between an opened screened door opening when going outside in case a lock locks accidentally. Sometime I turn up the heat to stay warmer and or wear a windbreaker with a hood inside my mobile home because (I am a baby) do not want to get sick.

Somebody might SAVE some cards received and use them by cutting the part written on off and sending the other

half of the cards back to the people that sent the whole cards? Somebody could save some better expensive ink pens that do not write to get replacement cartridges, or buy different new pens on sale, 24-pen pack from a store that is going out of business and closing for one-fifth the price of the new cartridges. Somebody could save some old school books for references and do some of the problems not assigned to strengthen those areas, and could get proper educational material to study from the LIBRARY instead of negative material.

If somebody leaves the garage door open an opossum or some other critter might be in an opened rubbish container waiting very impatiently for din-dins while fantasizing and assuming where usually the devil is, or trying to get out. Someone could spray the inside and outside of the containers with pest control plus germ destroyer. Someone could ATTACH the lids so they do not blow away into the street, lock the lids on, put the street address on the containers and lids, the containers should not be in view from the street, and might not put them out until next week because not much rubbish.

Somebody could use a mirror and a flashlight in a storage-shed to find a wasp nest during the cold weather while having on a warm jacket with a hood, gloves, and safety goggles, then spray wasp spray from a SAFE distance, and could wear a protective beehive hat in a garden to reduce insect stings at home if needed. An old window air conditioning unit that is cemented into a wall opening could be oiled for the two fan motor holes by freeing one end of eight side louvers, file down the sharp edges so can get a hand and an oil hose through the opening, use the oil hose for the old furnace two-fan motor holes, and vacuum the furnace.

Chapter 5 Other Helpful Ideas

A licensed electrician could put a warning ribbon on the outside of the fuse box stating DANGER MEN WORKING DO NOT TOUCH! The electrician could clean the circuit breaker contact points by turning off the main power, turn each circuit breaker switch off and on three times to remove some galvanic corrosion (metal with electricity), clean and tighten any loose fuses, do the requested work, and all electrical outlets by water faucets should be ground fault interrupted.

You could have more TIME to do things if REDUCING THE COMPLEXITY OF THINGS, and try to solve your problems, if not could ask for help from professional organizations IF having the time and money to do that. You have two weeks of vacation time to paint the outside of the house and your supplier from work offers to do that, so let him paint and spend that time on vacation with your family.

Somebody could buy a DYMO Embossing Label Maker with colored label tapes for home labeling and put identification tape around a few electrical cords of some small appliances in case they get misplaced. The label tape glue on the back of the colored tape is hard to remove from the different attached surfaces, which is definitely a very real big significant important considerable thing for some particular observable conscious people.

Someone could put hot water into a bowl and turn a jar upside down into the bowl so the lid will EXPAND to become easier to open with an eight ringed twist jar opener. Someone could fill the sinks and bathtub with hot water during the hot weather and drain them to help clean the inside of some pipes, and the faucet screens in the kitchen, bathroom, and shower as well as bathtub drain should be cleaned once in a while.

Somebody might have a helix plumbing wire cable pushed down the roof cleanout pipes to unblock them if needed.

I should get the old couch repaired and scotch guarded, but instead put some pillows and cushions under the couch cushions because the SEAT FRAME IS SINKING! I put some old sheets and clothes under my mattress to make it more level for more years because the TOP MIDDLE AREA IS SINKING. I attached the top sheet to the two end side lower corners of the mattress so the sheet does not move from the two attached positions, and left the blanket loose so can remove it easily if it becomes too warm.

Somebody should check if having the right kind of batteries for things and clean the contact points with 70 percent Isopropyl Rubbing Alcohol on a Q-tip for better efficiency, might remove a nickel-metal hydride battery from a radio and replace it with an alkaline battery if required, and remove batteries from things not being used. Two-tone heavy duty colored neoprene cotton knit lined GLOVES from ACE Hardware are comfortable to use, could use the gloves, pliers and a shop-vac vacuum cleaner to pick up the broken pieces if breaking a glass cup, or might buy eating and cooking ware that does not break when dropped.

Someone could put three-by-five cards, ink pen, pencil-pen or pencil in all suit jackets, coats, and jackets, and could put a paper pad and an ink pen by the bed to write notes so might sleep after writing the notes. If someone makes a long distance phone call and is put on HOLD could cost a lot of money. Someone is talking to somebody that is at a high position and wanting to shake off a person that is giving a hard time, and might tell the person in the high position that the person that is giving a hard time of a problem knows someone

that is in a higher position, but use good judgment because it might not work.

Someone could talk about the negative things on the phone with effective communications to shorten the phone calls, and if not wanting a friend to call back because of the hour of the day and type of phone call tell the friend, thanks for calling! Someone might tell somebody that is not a friend, not interested thanks anyway, or might have an ANSWERING MACHINE to review the phone calls.

Somebody might tell the installer of the mattress support frame to remove the mattress packaging and cardboard OUTSIDE FIRST, because wood crickets are in some packaging and can be three inches long. Somebody could spray the areas inside the home with home insect pest control where INSECTS seem to be coming from, like the perimeter by the floor baseboards, around glass windows, on the screens, and make a large X in the opened room carpeting area, better to fog inside and under the mobile home to destroy more insects, and spray the outside ground perimeter of the home as needed.

My anatomy SCALE for measuring: side of little finger one-half inch thick, thumb one-inch wide, forefinger three inches long, end of little finger to first wrist crease line six inches, outer shoe length one foot, arms stretched out horizontally to end of fingers six feet, and top of fingers from one hand stretched vertically above head eight feet. I have the left side of my haircut shorter up to the parting because the left side grows faster.

Somebody could use the thickest throw rugs by the kitchen and bathroom sinks for added comfort, and might take

some rugs to the Laundromat to have them professionally cleaned if having good backings. Somebody could shake the old rugs, vacuum them, use a real long pole handle with a brush at the end with a cleaning solution made in a pail to brush the top of the rugs. Somebody could pick up the noticeable pieces off the carpeting and rugs instead of vacuuming them. People should not have the refrigerator too close to a wall, or a rug too close to the front of the refrigerator which would reduce ventilation and might cause the refrigerator to make NOISES?

Someone could dust using a shop-vac vacuum cleaner, long handle brush, dust mitten, and a hair blower to vacuum the dust that is harder to reach, could use a long round small diameter appliance brush and a hair blower to loosen the dust before VACUUMING the refrigerator motor, and the area under the refrigerator every other year. Somebody might put frozen items temporarily into a storage-shed during the winter while cleaning the refrigerator and freezer, or might just move things and wipe the inside, and mark the date on a piece of tape.

Someone might buy a three-foot GRIPPER with two small rubber cups at the end that can pick up a paperclip to five pounds, and is handy for outside to pick up cigarette butts. Somebody might reverse the two-cup screws and lock them on with three tight nuts each, because if losing one of the cups the product will not function which is defiantly a very real big important considerable thing for some observable over conscious particular fastidious people like me.

People should keep some tools handy in the home for occasional inside repairs, use the RIGHT tools for the different kinds of repairs, and should check inside and outside of what was done, then put the tools used back in safe places or might lose some of them. Somebody might have old drills, saws,

scissors, and lawn mower blade sharpened by using a sharping stone for the lawn mower blade, and might not get things back if lending them while bothering their mind, or they might come back in three years as DAMAGED?

Someone could spray outside lawn insects and weeds early before they start to get bigger, and might shake their jacket before entering the home during the late spring weather of many very small energetic INSECTS that are hard to see. Somebody could have a firm brush mat to stand on by the front door for people to clean the bottom of their FOOTWEAR before entering the home, and could bring a pair of slippers when visiting a person's home. Someone could keep a scrub brush for the sides and bottom of their footwear, buffing brush, cloth, shoehorn, and a flathead screwdriver by a chair to remove pebbles from hiking shoes, and double knot shoelaces so they might not come undone. Someone might hang a bug zapper inside to eliminate some insects if needed in a vacation cabin by a scenic lake during the hot summer weather, could leave one light on inside of a room at night, and use Windex Glass Spray Cleaner and a flyswatter to reduce insects, or FOG them.

Socks size 9 to 12 are usually less so if needing size 10 probably better to buy 12 to 16, and socks should not be too tight over the calves. Somebody could wait to wash clothes until having food on them or smell some because washing and drying clothes too much shrinks them and fades the colors. Somebody might put pillows and cushions into the dryer to eliminate dust mites, and at a different time only outside work gloves to destroy bacteria. Somebody could put a cushion inside of four plastic bags and tape closed to protect from the dry and wet ground for SITTING on while doing repairs.

Chapter 5 Other Helpful Ideas

Somebody could cover a window air conditioning unit outside with a three-quarter-inch thick walled wood box, add caulking, weather-stripping, and a thick folded sheet inside to help keep the inside WARMER and QUITTER during the windy cold freezing weather, also if real windy and cold the temperature could drop 20° F during one hour. Someone should have a long handle broom, snow shovel, strong steel shovel for ice, an ice scraper on a long handle, and a rock salt container by the door ready for the next snowfall.

If having a problem try to get it resolved right away before it gets worse, even if only the garbage disposal is leaking on the floor. The GARBAGE DISPOSAL drainpipe could plug if any kind of the following goes down the disposal: glass, eggshells, coffee grounds, artichoke skins, corncobs, cantaloupe skins, or grease of any kind! Someone could review their product owner's manuals with store receipts attached for operation, care, maintenance, and warranty.

When the temperature progresses from the winter seasonal lowest temperature to the summer highest temperature might need to have some doors, locks, and windows ADJUSTED because of the different linear contractions and expansions of the different kinds of materials, and could have doors and windows installed for better fits at 50° F or so.

People could MULCH colorful leaves into the lawn instead of bagging them for a healthier lawn before they get too deep. People might use a lawnmower with a grass catcher to put the mulched leaves in a pile, then rake and scoop them into leaf bag openings with long rubber gloves. They could push the leaves down, put more of them into the bag openings, and store the bags in a dry place until ready to take them to the curb with a two wheel dooly.

Chapter 5 Other Helpful Ideas

Somebody might make a shuffleboard game used with cue V-sticks and round disks on the floor in a home basement or other area, and might plant a nice garden in June which is usually a favorable time for some adequate soiled areas. Someone could use outdoor Silicone Water Shield Spray from the camping department or semi odorless Scotch Guard Fabric Protector for coats, jackets, hats, gloves, both sides of umbrellas, some footwear, tote bags, athletic gym bags, vehicle floor mats, trunk carpeting, and a tent, then leave them in the storage-shed for two days if used outdoor Silicone Water Shield Spray because of ODORS.

Buildings could have two heavily armed SECURITY GUARDS inside and outside, and more concerts could be in buildings for security. Voting could be at the age of TWENTY-EIGHT when the brain is mostly developed. Elections could have minimum education and maximum age limit requirements with step aside maximum age limit for some positions. People that have a computer should clean the bottom of the computer mouse, and computers could make more of the decisions because of DECEPTION, GREED, and MISMANAGEMENT of money for a SMOOTHER continuous government instead of by elections and voting to reduce protests in this Unfair Deceptive Cold Stained Busy System of Things which is: NOT GETTING GOOD information, advice, EDUCATION, mentoring, counseling, tutoring, or follow-up EARLY IN LIFE and later on, being uninformed, DECEPTION, greed, verbal and physical abuse, LACK OF BETTER EDUCATION, COMMUNICATIONS, religion, ethics, time, money, and love!

Chapter 5 Other Helpful Ideas

Everybody can profit from the variety of the diversification of some of these many HELPFUL IDEAS, some more, some less depending on their experiences in life. You could do this, should do that, or you might do something else different, good luck.

www.ingramcontent.com/pod-product-compliance
Ingram Content Group UK Ltd.
Pitfield, Milton Keynes, MK11 3LW, UK
UKHW020138250726
13967UKWH00002B/731